BRIGHT
IDEA
BOOKS

LUPITA
Nyong'o

by Stephanie Watson

DISCARD

CAPSTONE PRESS
a capstone imprint

Bright Ideas is published by Capstone Press, an imprint of Capstone.
1710 Roe Crest Drive
North Mankato, Minnesota 56003
www.capstonepub.com

Library of Congress Cataloging-in-Publication Data
Names: Watson, Stephanie, 1969- author.
Title: Lupita Nyong'o / by Stephanie Watson.
Description: North Mankato, Minnesota : Capstone Press, [2020] | Series: Influential People | Includes index. | Audience: Grades: 4-6
Identifiers: LCCN 2019029530 (print) | LCCN 2019029531 (ebook) | ISBN 9781543590760 (hardcover) | ISBN 9781496665850 (paperback) | ISBN 9781543590777 (ebook)
Subjects: LCSH: Nyong'o, Lupita—Juvenile literature. | Actors—Kenya—Biography—Juvenile literature. | Actors, Black—Mexico—Biography—Juvenile literature.
Classification: LCC PN2991.8.N96 W38 2020 (print) | LCC PN2991.8.N96 (ebook) | DDC 791.43092—dc23
LC record available at https://lccn.loc.gov/2019029530
LC ebook record available at https://lccn.loc.gov/2019029531

Image Credits
AP Images: Dave Bedrosian/Geisler-Fotopress/picture-alliance/dpa, cover, Matt Sayles/Invision, 6–7; Rex Features: Jaap Buitendijk/Focus Features/Kobal, 15, Marion Curtis/Starpix, 10, Moviestore, 21, Warner Bros/Kobal, 13; Shutterstock Images: Debby Wong, 16, Dfree, 27, Featureflash Photo Agency, 24–25, Jaguar PS, 5, Kathy Hutchins, 19, 22, 28, Sopotnicki, 9, wavebreakmedia, 31
Design Elements: Shutterstock Images

Editorial Credits
Editor: Charly Haley; Designer: Laura Graphenteen; Production Specialist: Colleen McLaren

Printed in the United States of America.
PA99

TABLE OF CONTENTS

CHAPTER ONE
THE ACADEMY AWARDS..... 4

CHAPTER TWO
GROWING UP 8

CHAPTER THREE
WORKING WITH HOLLYWOOD DREAMS........ 14

CHAPTER FOUR
SUPERSTAR 20

Glossary 28
Timeline............................. 29
Activity 30
Further Resources............... 32
Index................................. 32

CHAPTER 1

THE ACADEMY
Awards

Lupita Nyong'o stood onstage. She wore a long blue dress. She held a golden trophy.

She looked out at the crowd. Everyone was standing. They clapped and cheered for her.

It was the 2014 Academy Awards. She won an award. It was for her first movie **role**. She played the character Patsey in *12 Years a Slave*.

Lupita Nyong'o showed off her Academy Award.

She spoke to the crowd. She thanked other people who worked on the movie. She thanked her family.

Then she had a message
for children around the world.
She said their dreams matter.
She cried as she spoke.
Everyone cheered again.

Nyong'o spoke to the crowd at the 2014 Academy Awards.

CHAPTER 2

GROWING Up

Nyong'o was born in Mexico City in 1983. Her parents are from Kenya in Africa. They moved back there after she was born. She grew up in Nairobi in Kenya. She has five brothers and sisters.

Nyong'o grew up in the city of Nairobi.

KENYAN CONNECTIONS

Nyong'o has family in the Luo **tribe** in Kenya. Former U.S. president Barack Obama also has family from this tribe.

Nyong'o has always
loved acting.

ACTING

Nyong'o went to a school for all girls. She loved acting. She performed skits at family parties.

She tried out for a play when she was 14 years old. It was *Romeo and Juliet.* It was at a small theater. She got the lead role of Juliet.

Nyong'o wanted to be a famous actor. She liked watching American television. But she rarely saw women with dark skin like hers in movies. She prayed for lighter skin.

Then she saw *The Color Purple*. The women in the movie had dark skin. She saw she could be like them. She could be a famous actor too.

Whoopi Goldberg in
The Color Purple

CHAPTER 3

WORKING WITH
Hollywood
Dreams

Nyong'o moved to the United States in 2003. She went to college to study film.

She worked on a movie during one of her summer breaks. The movie was called *The Constant Gardener.* It was filmed near her home in Nairobi. She did not act. She helped behind the scenes.

A scene from *The Constant Gardener*, starring Rachel Weisz (left) and Ralph Fiennes

Nyong'o has worked on many different film projects.

Nyong'o moved back to Nairobi after college. She got her first big acting role in 2009. She starred in the TV show *Shuga*. It was on MTV in Africa.

That same year she made a movie. It was called *In My Genes*. It was about people with **albinism**. They have no color in their skin and hair. The movie showed how badly they were treated in Kenya.

Nyong'o wanted to be a better actor. She moved back to the United States. She went to Yale University.

She graduated in 2012. She got the role in *12 Years a Slave* that same year.

Nyong'o has become very famous in the United States.

CHAPTER 4

SUPERSTAR

12 Years a Slave made Nyong'o a star. She once feared her dark skin would stop her from acting. Now she was famous. She even won an **Oscar**.

Nyong'o (left) in
12 Years a Slave

Nyong'o is now famous for more than acting.

Nyong'o also became a model. She modeled for a famous makeup company. She has been in ads and magazines.

MOST BEAUTIFUL

People magazine named Nyong'o its "Most Beautiful" person in 2014.

STARRING ROLES

Nyong'o got many roles after *12 Years a Slave*. She played Maz Kanata in a Star Wars movie. She was the voice of the wolf Raksha in *The Jungle Book*. She played Nakia in *Black Panther*.

Nyong'o (third from left) and the stars of *Black Panther*

She got a star on the Hollywood Walk of Fame in 2019. She was 36 years old.

HELPING OTHERS

Nyong'o uses her fame to help others. She supports groups that help animals.

She also supports other black women. She speaks out about how black women are often treated badly. For one magazine photo shoot she wore her hair in a ponytail. The magazine erased her ponytail in the photo. She was mad that the magazine changed her hair. She believes women do not need to change to be beautiful.

Nyong'o speaks out for what she believes in.

albinism
a condition in which a person is born without color in their skin and hair

Oscar
a famous award given to someone who works in film, also called an Academy Award

role
a part in a TV show, movie, or play

tribe
a group of people, often with a similar background, who usually live in the same area and have a leader

TIMELINE

1983: Lupita Nyong'o is born in Mexico City, Mexico, on March 1.

2003: Nyong'o moves to the United States.

2009: Nyong'o writes and directs the documentary *In My Genes*.

2009-2012: Nyong'o stars in the MTV show *Shuga*.

2014: Nyong'o wins an Oscar for *12 Years a Slave* on March 2.

2019: Nyong'o gets a star on the Hollywood Walk of Fame.

ACTIVITY

MAKE A COLLAGE

Create a collage of people you admire. You can cut out their photos from magazines, or you can print out their photos off of the internet. While deciding who to include in your collage, you can ask questions like:

- What are their careers?

- Why do they inspire you?

- What good have they done in the world?

- How are they similar to or different from each other?

FURTHER RESOURCES

Nyong'o wrote a book for children. Check it out:

Nyong'o, Lupita. *Sulwe.* New York: Simon & Schuster, 2018.

Want to learn more about actors from *Black Panther*? Check out these books:

McManus, Celina. *Michael B. Jordan.* North Mankato, Minn.: Capstone Press, 2020.

Zalewski, Aubrey. *Chadwick Boseman.* North Mankato, Minn.: Capstone Press, 2020.

Interested in acting? Check out these websites:

Wonderopolis: Can Anyone Be an Actor?
https://wonderopolis.org/wonder/can-anyone-be-an-actor

Wonderopolis: How Do You Become Famous?
https://wonderopolis.org/wonder/how-do-you-become-famous

INDEX

acting, 5, 11–12, 17–18, 20, 24
albinism, 17

Black Panther, 24

Hollywood Walk of Fame, 25

magazines, 23, 26
modeling, 23
movies, 5–6, 12, 15, 17, 24

Nairobi, Kenya, 8, 15, 17

12 Years a Slave, 5, 18, 20, 24

Yale University, 18

7

BRIGHT IDEA BOOKS

When Lupita Nyong'o was a young girl, she didn't think she could be a famous actor. Now she is an Academy Award winner. Learn more about her rise to stardom!

BOOKS IN THIS SERIES

LeBron James
Lupita Nyong'o
Maddie Ziegler
Michael B. Jordan
Millie Bobby Brown
Stephen Curry

capstone
capstonepub.com

ISBN 978-1-
50795

9 781496 665850